Scientists IN ACTION

GEOLOGISTS IN ACTION

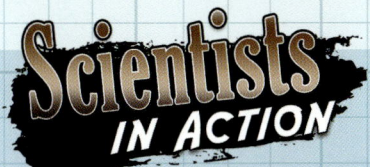

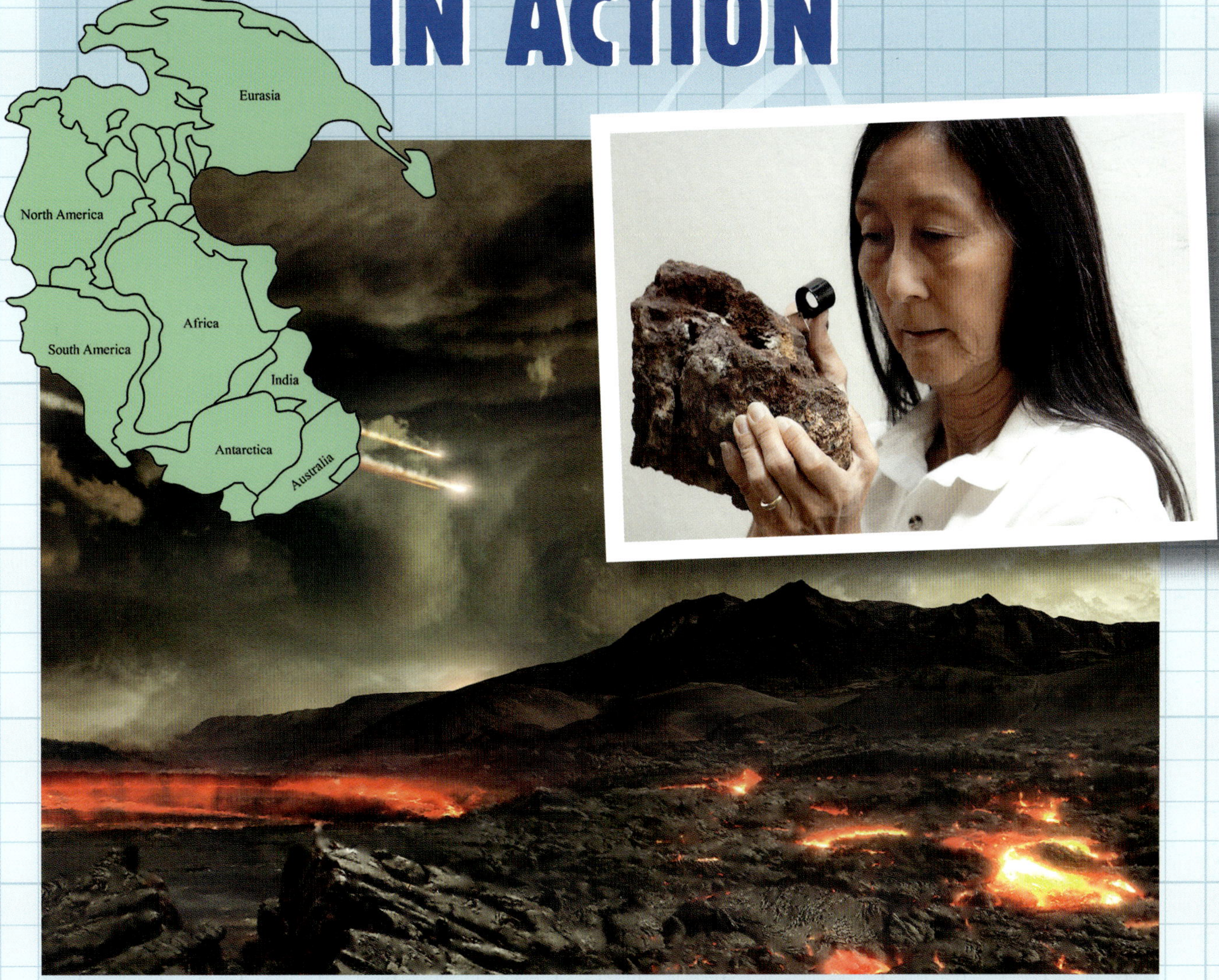

CRABTREE
PUBLISHING COMPANY
WWW.CRABTREEBOOKS.COM

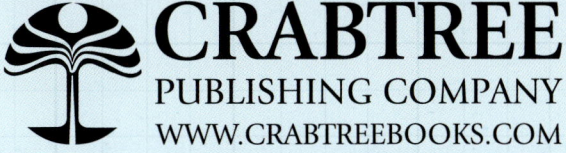

James Bow

Author: James Bow

Series research and development: Reagan Miller

Editorial director: Kathy Middleton

Photo research: James Nixon

Editors: Paul Humphrey, James Nixon, Reagan Miller

Proofreader and indexer: Lorna Notsch

Designer: Keith Williams (sprout.uk.com)

Prepress technician: Samara Parent

Print coordinator: Katherine Berti

Illustrator: Keith Williams (sprout.uk.com)

Consultant: Brianne Manning

Produced for Crabtree Publishing Company by Discovery Books

Cover image: A geologist collects active lava samples from Kilauea, a volcano in Hawaii

Photographs:

Alamy: pp. 5 bottom (Vladimir Smirnov/TASS/Alamy Live News); 10 (Olaf Doering); 11 (Keith Douglas); 12 (Greenshoots Communications); 14 (Arctic Images); 15 (Aurora Photos); 16 bottom (RGB Ventures/SuperStock); 18 bottom (Bill Bachman); 20 (Frederic Cholin); 22 (Stefan Sauer/dpa picture alliance); 23 top (John Cancalosi); 25 left (MshieldsPhotos)

Getty Images: p. 28 (CHRISTIAN MIRANDA/AFP)

Pixnio: p. 21 top (Gari Mayberry/USAID)

U.S. Geological Survey: pp. title page top right, 4, 13 (Thomas Reiss/USGS Pacific Coastal and Marine Science Center); 19 (Amy West)

Wikimedia: cover (Hawaii Volcano Observatory, USGS); pp. 5 top (Brocken Inaglory); 6-7 bottom (NASA's Goddard Space Flight Center Conceptual Image Lab); 8 top and bottom; 9 top (Ian Freeman); 9 bottom (Eugene Cernan/NASA); 16 top (Hannes Grobe/AWI); 17 (Natalino Russo/ESA); 18 top (James St. John); 21 bottom; 23 bottom (Biswarup Ganguly); 24 (NOAA); 25 right (NASA); 26 (Mark A. Wilson); 29 top (Tulane Public Relations); 29 bottom (NASA/JPL)

All other images from Shutterstock

Library and Archives Canada Cataloguing in Publication

Bow, James, 1972-, author
    Geologists in action / James Bow.

(Scientists in action)
Includes index.
Issued in print and electronic formats.
ISBN 978-0-7787-4653-9 (hardcover).--
ISBN 978-0-7787-4657-7 (softcover).--
ISBN 978-1-4271-2061-8 (HTML)

    1. Geology--Juvenile literature. 2. Geologists--Juvenile literature.
I. Title.

QE29.B684 2018   j551   C2017-907813-5
                                                                           C2017-907814-3

Library of Congress Cataloging-in-Publication Data

Names: Bow, James, author.
Title: Geologists in action / James Bow.
Description: New York, New York : Crabtree Publishing, [2018] | Series: Scientists in action | Includes index.
Identifiers: LCCN 2018000102 (print) | LCCN 2018006698 (ebook) | ISBN 9781427120618 (Electronic) | ISBN 9780778746539 (hardcover : alk. paper) | ISBN 9780778746577 (pbk. : alk. paper)
Subjects: LCSH: Geology--Juvenile literature. | Geologists--Juvenile literature.
Classification: LCC QE29 (ebook) | LCC QE29 .B6825 2018 (print) | DDC 551--dc23
LC record available at https://lccn.loc.gov/2018000102

Crabtree Publishing Company
www.crabtreebooks.com   1-800-387-7650

Printed in the U.S.A./052018/CG20180309

Copyright © 2018 CRABTREE PUBLISHING COMPANY. All rights reserved. No part of this publication may be reproduced, stored in a retrieval system or be transmitted in any form or by any means, electronic, mechanical, photocopying, recording, or otherwise, without the prior written permission of Crabtree Publishing Company. In Canada: We acknowledge the financial support of the Government of Canada through the Canada Book Fund for our publishing activities.

Published in Canada
Crabtree Publishing
616 Welland Ave.
St. Catharines, Ontario
L2M 5V6

Published in the United States
Crabtree Publishing
PMB 59051
350 Fifth Avenue, 59th Floor
New York, New York 10118

Published in the United Kingdom
Crabtree Publishing
Maritime House
Basin Road North, Hove
BN41 1WR

Published in Australia
Crabtree Publishing
3 Charles Street
Coburg North
VIC, 3058

CONTENTS

Geologists in Action	4
The Big Questions	6
What Geologists Have Learned So Far	8
Scientific Investigation	10
Asking Questions	12
Planning Investigations	14
The Geologist's Toolbox	16
Analyzing Data	18
Drawing Conclusions	20
Communicate Your Findings	22
Peer Review	24
Investigating Landslides	26
The Future of the Field	28
Learning More	30
Glossary	31
Index & About the Author	32

GEOLOGISTS IN ACTION

Imagine standing next to the opening of an active volcano. Sharp, black rocks surround you, while others smoke or glow red hot. Using a pair of long, metal tongs, you scoop up a sample of glowing, liquid rock. The mountain rumbles. It's dangerous, but your sample will help other scientists learn more about the volcano. It could help predict future eruptions, saving thousands of lives. This could be you, if you were a geologist.

This geologist is taking a sample of hot lava using a long cable.

What Are Geologists?

Geology is the study of Earth. Scientists who study geology are called geologists. Within this vast field, geologists study such different topics as: What causes earthquakes? Why do mountains rise and fall? What was Earth like millions of years ago? Geologists study rocks. They look for clues that help them understand and predict events, such as volcanic eruptions, landslides, and floods. They study the structure of the ground beneath our feet, helping people find energy reserves and underground water supplies. They also study ancient **organisms**, through **fossils**, to understand how Earth has changed over time, and how it might change in the future.

Scientists do not know what caused these unusual holes in the rocks at Point Lobos in California. Geologists seek to solve mysteries such as this.

Studying Scientists

In this book, we will look at how geologists study Earth, the questions they've answered, and the questions they are still trying to solve. We will also examine how geologists use scientific practices to guide their investigations and make discoveries in their field.

From the Field: Stephen Sparks

British geologist Stephen Sparks studies volcanoes all around the world. Sparks studied the **theory** that an eruption in the Aegean Sea around 1500 B.C.E. destroyed the Minoan civilization on the island of Crete, in Greece. Sparks analyzed, or closely studied, samples of deep-sea rocks and fossils near the volcano. He found that the eruption was much more powerful than previously thought. Sparks was recently awarded the Vetlesen Prize, considered to be the Nobel Prize for geologists.

Learning about Earth often means going out and studying it directly.

5

THE BIG QUESTIONS

All branches of science have questions that scientists are working to answer. Geology is no different. Here are some questions that are puzzling geologists.

What Is Happening beneath Earth's Surface?

Geologists peel back the layers of Earth. The surface, called the crust, is up to 18.6 miles (30 kilometers) thick and is divided into chunks called plates. These plates float on the **mantle**, where heat and pressure melt rock into a liquid called magma. At the center of the planet is an iron core. The outer core is liquid, whereas the smaller inner core is under so much pressure that it is solid. **Currents** of hotter magma rising from the lower mantle toward the crust push the floating plates together or pull them apart. These movements cause earthquakes and create volcanoes. However, geologists aren't sure why magma currents exist.

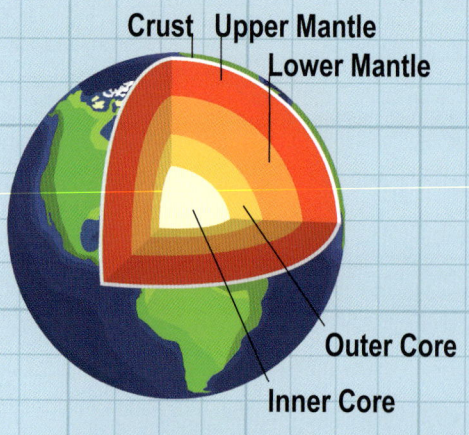

What Happened during the Early Earth?

The oldest rocks on Earth date from 4 billion years ago, but scientists believe the planet was formed 4.54 billion years ago, when dust in the ancient solar system clumped together to form large planets. Without any direct **evidence**, geologists are curious to find out what took place on Earth in those first 500 million years, called Earth's "Dark Age."

Geologists believe the early Earth had a surface of molten rock and was struck by asteroids.

What Can Geology Tell Us about Climate Change?

By studying the fossils of ancient plants and animals, geologists can tell whether the climate at the time the organisms were alive was hot, cold, wet, or dry. These clues have revealed an Earth that has at times had forests in Antarctica and snow at the equator. Geology offers historical evidence to help answer questions, such as how much Earth's climate can change, and how fast.

More than Just the Study of Rocks

There are two main branches of geology. **Physical geology** studies what Earth is made of and how it works. This includes:

Geochemistry: the study of what Earth's crust is made of

Geophysics: the study of why Earth acts the way it does

Hydrogeology: the study of how water underground and on the surface shapes the planet

Oceanography: the study of the ocean floor

Structural geology: the study of how the Earth's crust is layered, and how those layers form

Volcanology: the study of volcanoes and what powers them

The other branch of geology is **historical geology**, which studies the history of Earth through its rocks, including:

Paleontology: the study of organisms that lived in **prehistoric** times

Petrology: the study of how rocks are formed and are changed over time

WHAT GEOLOGISTS HAVE LEARNED SO FAR

Geologists' understanding of Earth has changed over time, thanks to research and experiments. Here are some of the big discoveries made in the field.

The Age of Earth

Scottish geologist Charles Lyell (1797–1875) studied volcanoes, fossils, and the shape and structure of certain rocks. Knowing how long it took for rocks to be made and **eroded**, he decided that Earth was far older than people had previously believed. He published *The Principles of Geology* to explain his theories, and supported other scientists' theories, such as Charles Darwin's theory of **evolution**.

Charles Lyell

Continental Drift

In 1912, German geophysicist Alfred Wegener looked at a map and saw that South America looked like it could fit next to Africa like jigsaw puzzle pieces. He believed that all the continents might once have fitted together and had been pushed apart to their current positions. Other geologists at the time rejected his theory. However, in 1968, geoscientist Jack Oliver, studying the vibrations of deep earthquakes, explained the processes that could drive plates and continents apart. This theory came to be known as **plate tectonics**, or continental drift.

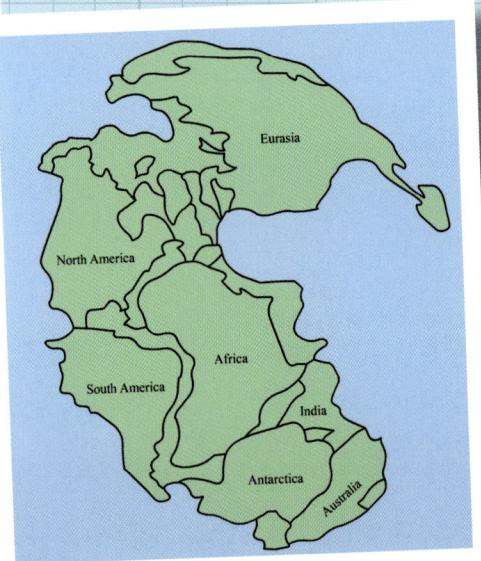

Geologists believe that, 270 million years ago, all the continents of Earth were joined together in a supercontinent called Pangaea.

Earth's Climate Changes

In 1837, Swiss geologist and biologist Louis Agassiz (1807–1873) was dating fossils when he noticed that a number of species suddenly went extinct at roughly the same time. This led him to a theory that Earth had been gripped by a sudden **ice age** thousands of years before. Other geologists found evidence to support this in **sedimentary rock** deposits and fossilized **tree rings**. Evidence now suggests the Northern Hemisphere has experienced at least four major ice ages in the past million years.

Geologists continue to make new discoveries. Indeed, many discoveries spark more questions, which lead to new research and more discoveries.

Fossilized tree stumps can provide clues to geologists about what happened on Earth millions of years ago.

This photo shows Harrison Schmitt collecting rock samples from the moon.

Geologists in Space!

Harrison Schmitt was the first geologist in space. He went to the moon on the *Apollo 17* spacecraft and brought back moon rocks for geologists to look at. By comparing Earth to other moons and planets, geologists help spot clues that suggest whether life may exist there. Robot probes sent to Mars and some asteroids have also collected samples. Geologists have found evidence that Mars had water on its surface in the past. Where there's water, there may be life.

SCIENTIFIC INVESTIGATION

There is no precise step-by-step process for scientific investigation. However, all scientific investigations share similar practices (see box), which makes sure that the conclusions reached are supported by facts.

The Search for Answers

As with other fields of science, geological discoveries start with a question. For example, why are earthquakes happening in a certain area? To answer their question, geologists put forward and then test potential answers called **hypotheses**. They make observations and plan and carry out experiments, gathering data to test each hypothesis. Interpreting the data, they build an explanation for what they are seeing, and then they offer this explanation to other scientists. This explanation is tested and debated, and better explanations often result.

Scientific Practices
- Asking questions
- Developing methods of investigation, including building **models** and designing observations and experiments
- Carrying out investigations
- Analyzing and **interpreting** data collected
- Using mathematics and technology to process data
- Constructing explanations from evidence
- Communicating findings and conclusions

Geologists sometimes work in laboratories, using chemicals or machines to see what particular rocks or soils are made out of, how strong they are, and how they react to certain chemicals.

A geologist investigates the rock on Hudson Bay Mountain, British Columbia.

Lab Experiments vs. Field Observations

Some scientists conduct experiments in laboratories to test their hypotheses and gather evidence. In laboratories, scientists often use a "control." They take something being analyzed and split it up, keeping one part (the control) unchanged. By experimenting on the other parts, they can compare the changes against the control.

Most geologists, however, carry out their investigations in the field, where a control isn't possible. They go out into the natural world to make observations and gather their evidence. They visit volcanoes and collect readings on how hot things are underground. They return to rivers to see how rocks are being eroded over time. They measure earthquakes and log when they happened, where they occurred, and how powerful they were. They get data from **sonar** ships or orbiting **satellites** to map the ocean floor.

From the data they retrieve, geologists can build models of what they are observing. These can be real models or computer simulations. They can run tests on these models to see how they react to certain changes, such as drilling or increased magma pressure.

Scientific investigation is not always a straightforward process. Parts are often repeated, with explanations tested and re-tested, sometimes over years, before the answers become clear and are accepted by the wider scientific community.

ASKING QUESTIONS

Since geologists' field of study is Earth, they ask questions about the world around them. How was Earth formed? What is it made of? Where and when will earthquakes strike next? How has land around a river or a lake eroded?

Exploring for Oil

Sometimes the questions are very specific, such as where are deposits of oil, **minerals**, or metals? Petroleum geology is the study of **fossil fuels** and where to find them. Fossil fuels are the remains of plants and animals buried millions of years ago beneath layers of rock. Heat and pressure have changed them into coal, oil, and natural gas.

To find these deposits, petroleum geologists have to ask a number of questions. Are the layers of rock arranged in such a way that these deposits can be trapped? Are the rock layers old enough that natural gas, oil, or coal can have formed? How much oil, coal, or natural gas is there likely to be? Where is the best place to drill or mine? Each question requires its own investigation, and the answers spark further investigations as energy companies search for new sources of fossil fuels.

A geologist in Mali, Africa, surveys the land in his search for oil.

More Questions than Answers

Sometimes, research provides more questions than answers. Our understanding of plate tectonics, earthquakes, and volcanoes has improved over the past few decades, but we still have a long way to go in predicting exactly when earthquakes will strike. In the early 1990s, geologists looking at the patterns of previous earthquakes predicted one would strike Parkfield, California, in 1994. Unfortunately, the earthquake didn't strike until 10 years later. However, in science, even failed predictions are helpful, because they allow scientists to ask why the result wasn't what they expected. Following these questions helps us better understand the world and how it works.

From the Field: Carol Hirozawa-Reiss

Carol Hirozawa-Reiss is a marine geologist for the U.S. Geological Survey. She studies the geology of the ocean floor in a submarine more than 1.25 miles (2 kilometers) beneath the surface. She is studying the Juan de Fuca ridge off the coast of Washington State, where two tectonic plates are pulling apart. The U.S. Geological Survey wants to find out how fast the plates are separating. Farther to the east, the Juan de Fuca plate is being pushed under the North American plate, causing earthquakes and building volcanoes. Measuring the plates' movements will help scientists understand the forces that are building up near the cities of Portland and Seattle.

Carol Hirozawa-Reiss analyzes a sample of rock from the bottom of the ocean.

PLANNING INVESTIGATIONS

After asking the question, scientists investigate potential answers. Scientists will often make a hypothesis. Geologists then have to decide where and how to look for clues, which will prove or challenge their hypothesis.

Searching for the Sea

Geologist Erich Osterberg is working with a team of scientists in the Trans-Antarctic Mountains to see if Antarctica was ice-free 125,000 years ago. As scientists investigate global climate change, one question they ask is "How has Earth's climate changed in the past?" Osterberg's team is drilling into the ice, collecting samples that formed around that time. The Trans-Antarctic Mountains are hundreds of miles away from any ocean, so why investigate here? Because the land beneath this part of the Antarctic ice cap is below sea level. If the model is true and the ice cap had melted completely, this would prove that the Trans-Antarctic Mountains once formed a coastline.

Getting samples from underground or under ice requires heavy drilling.

Hunting down the Clues

Planning an investigation means knowing where to go, what to look for, and in some cases, who to talk to. Some geologists look at the fossil record. If a number of animal or plant species became extinct at the same time, this may suggest that a huge disaster took place. Other geologists find clues in the landscape from patterns of erosion, such as boulders swept into strange places, or silt laid down in normally dry fields. These findings would suggest ancient floods. Oral histories told by local people can alert geologists to something that happened, which scientists at the time did not record.

From the Field: Brian Atwater

Geologist Brian Atwater, working for the U.S. Geological Survey, investigated the possibility that a major earthquake and a **tsunami** hit the Pacific Northwest in the year 1700. He and his team searched the coast, noticing that a number of old trees appeared to have died at the same time. The oral history of the local **Indigenous** people talked about the ground shaking and a giant wave sweeping away villages. Across the Pacific Ocean, records from 1700 mentioned a surprise tsunami that struck Japan, even though no earthquake had been felt. He wrote up his investigation in the book *The Orphan Tsunami of 1700* and warned that a strong earthquake and possible tsunami could hit the area again within the next 50 years.

Brian Atwater collects samples from a mud bank at low tide as part of his investigation into a tsunami in 1700.

THE GEOLOGIST'S TOOLBOX

Like all scientists, geologists must gather data to test their hypotheses. Geologists' data is often buried within Earth itself, and that doesn't make for easy data gathering. Sometimes, the thing they want to study is deep underground, like a reserve of oil, or a deep **fault line**. Geologists often get their hands dirty getting the data and need special tools to analyze it.

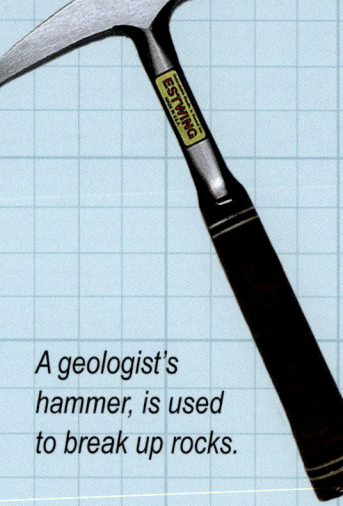

A geologist's hammer, is used to break up rocks.

Digging Deeper

On the surface, geologists gather samples using hammers, chisels, and brushes to chip away at and clean rock. Equipment like saws and polishers allow geologists to cut, carve, and shine rocks. Drills can dig deeper and bring up **core samples** of layered rock. To see deeper than this, geologists must "look through" the rock. This sounds impossible, but they do this by measuring vibrations called **seismic** waves. By measuring how fast these waves travel from earthquakes, geologists can build a map of the layers of rock underground.

This geologist is installing a seismic station to monitor earthquakes deep underground.

Geologists need to stay safe while collecting samples in the field. They often have to climb mountains or go through caves, and need the equipment for these tasks. Boots, knee pads, and helmets protect them against rugged terrain. Goggles protect their eyes when they're hammering or sawing away at samples. Reflective vests make sure they're easy to see, and portable shelters protect geologists in the field from the elements.

Once geologists have their samples, they have to observe and analyze them. Cameras can take pictures of things they can't carry home. Microscopes can look closer at the samples to see crystals and other structures. Geologists use acids and other chemicals to figure out what the samples are made of. Computers are a great help in recording, calculating, and analyzing data, but geologists also rely on notepads and clipboards to log their observations.

Caves often provide geological samples that haven't been disturbed for millions of years. These geologists are launching a drone with a camera to explore an area impossible for humans to reach.

Shining a Light on Rocks

A **spectrograph** works by shining white light on a sample and measuring its reflection. Different chemicals will reflect light differently, and this way, geologists can understand what a sample, like a rock, is made of. Volcanologists use this to analyze volcanic lava. By measuring the presence of dissolved water or **carbon dioxide**, they can tell when gases are building up in a volcano, possibly predicting an eruption.

ANALYZING DATA

The data geologists collect is meaningless until it is analyzed and interpreted. Geologists look for patterns in their observations or models and ask questions about what they find.

For example, in the early 20th century, geologists noticed that certain volcanic rocks acted like the magnet of a compass. Strangely, the magnets in different rocks were not pointing in the same direction. Some even pointed south when others were pointing north. What could cause these differences? As our understanding of Earth's **magnetic field** improved, scientists realized that the planets **magnetic poles** shift over time, sometimes even reversing. This understanding gave geologists something else—a timeline of when the magnetic rocks were formed.

Geologists analyze the minerals within rock samples.

Core samples are carefully stored and catalogued for future analysis.

Seeing the Patterns

Geologists know how certain rocks are formed, how they erode, and why the landscape takes on the shape it does. These patterns tell them what happened in Earth's prehistoric past. They also show geologists where oil and gas deposits are; where volcanic eruptions, earthquakes, tsunamis, or floods have happened in the past; and even where asteroids have struck.

Geologists assess and interpret data to see whether it supports their hypothesis. Scientists are open to receiving data that counters their hypothesis, because it advances our understanding of the world.

Computers can produce "difference maps." The red areas show where soil has been eroded, and the blue areas show where soil has been added by the flow of water.

J. Harlen Bretz's Outrageous Hypothesis

In the 1920s, American geologist J. Harlen Bretz analyzed the landscape near Spokane, Washington, noting large grooves in the exposed rock and boulders that were miles away from where they formed. He hypothesized that **cataclysmic** floods had swept over the state 14,000 years ago. He argued that the flood carried more than 10 times the flow of all the rivers on Earth.

Scientists at the time rejected his hypothesis, asking where all the water could have come from. However, over the next 40 years, geologists found other evidence that supported the flood theory. Even after scientists accepted the evidence, it wasn't until 1999 that a possible source for all that water—a giant lake, called Lake Missoula, held back by an ice dam—was identified. The floods are now known as the Missoula Floods.

DRAWING CONCLUSIONS

A hypothesis is an educated prediction that explains the known facts, but it is not the final answer. The results of the investigation lead scientists to decide whether the hypothesis is proven or disproven by the data. Whatever the result, the scientists have taken a step toward finding the correct answer.

Modeling the Results

After collecting data using sensors like **seismographs**, photographs, and maps, geologists build models of an area to see what this information can tell them. This can be an actual 3-D model, a computer model, or a map of the layers of rock beneath the surface. This model helps geologists see the patterns of Earth. It helps them identify the locations of plate boundaries and fault lines, or different layers of rock where oil, natural gas, or valuable minerals can be found. Geologists test and upgrade their models as new data comes in. Sometimes data can show that a model is wrong, but that's still valuable. It helps scientists to correct their model, improving their answers to the questions they hope to solve.

Geologists use charts to analyze the layers of rock, which helps them reach conclusions.

Analyzing the ash from a volcano helps geologists to predict future eruptions.

Where Did the Dinosaurs Go?

In 1980, geologist Walter Alvarez looked at the dinosaur fossils in museums and wondered why the creatures became extinct. Since the 19th century, paleontologists knew that these large reptiles roamed Earth until 65 million years ago. They weren't sure why they disappeared, however.

Alvarez noticed a streak in sedimentary rock samples dating from 65 million years ago. This streak showed up in samples all around the world. Analyzing the samples in his laboratory, he discovered this streak contained 100 times more **iridium** than was normal. Iridium is rare in Earth's crust, so Alvarez hypothesized that the iridium must have been brought from space by a large asteroid, and the effects of this asteroid strike caused the dinosaurs to go extinct.

Alvarez and his team gathered evidence to make the case. They even found a giant **crater**. The effects of an asteroid strike might or might not have killed the dinosaurs, but most scientists now agree that there definitely was a strike by a giant asteroid. It was 6 miles (10 kilometers) across, and it struck 65 million years ago, in what is now Mexico.

COMMUNICATE YOUR FINDINGS

A scientific discovery that isn't shared with other scientists is not science—at least, not yet. Like all scientists, geologists must check their findings, comparing their research to other research and making sure the results are accurate. Experiments are repeated and new observations made. Only when the results are repeated is a discovery considered true. So, when geologists have asked their questions and analyzed their observations, they need to report their conclusions to other scientists.

A geologist presents his discovery—a 250-million-year-old fossil of a prehistoric flying reptile. Fossils tell a lot about the changes to Earth's ancient climate.

Time to Report

When writing a report, scientists explain what they were investigating, the procedure they followed to do their research, the data they acquired, and whether that data supports or disproves their initial hypothesis. Scientists also describe work that took place in the area beforehand, the data those studies found, and the observations already made. Good science is science that other scientists can test and repeat.

The reporting scientist must also name who asked for the report, and who is funding their investigation. This is important to prevent groups who might want a particular result from adding **bias** to the science, or at least highlight where bias could come from. Businesses may want the reports on how a river valley erodes to downplay the impact of a development. Some energy companies may have downplayed reports that show **fracking** may contaminate groundwater and cause earthquakes.

A geologist examines the shale rock that may hold natural gas, before she reports her conclusions.

From the Field: Iain Simpson Stewart

Scottish geologist Iain Simpson Stewart has been described as geology's "rock star." A professor at the University of Plymouth, England, he has studied major earthquakes, volcanic eruptions, and tsunamis in the Mediterranean Sea. He is best known as a television presenter, producing and starring in a number of science documentaries such as Journeys from the Centre of the Earth, Rise of the Continents, and Fracking: The New Energy Rush, explaining geological concepts like plate tectonics and energy exploration.

PEER REVIEW

Geologists collaborate, meaning that they work together and share their discoveries. Research data from one project increases the knowledge of the field in general. This allows other researchers to find ways to make new discoveries. The work of the reporting scientist is studied and often challenged by other scientists. This is sometimes called peer review.

A Harsh Debate

Peer review can be a tough time for a scientist. When Alfred Wegener published his theory of continental drift, his idea was dismissed. How could continents move around the world? However, in the years that followed, other scientists gathered evidence that supported Wegener's theory. In 1952, a U.S. navy geologist named Marie Tharp analyzed sonar readings that revealed the Mid-Atlantic Ridge—a chain of undersea mountains larger and more vast than the Himalayas.

Analyzing the age of the rocks showed that the Atlantic Ocean was splitting here, and driving the surrounding continents apart. The data, when peer reviewed, was shown to be accurate. So, despite the ridicule of Wegener's peers, scientists later gathered the evidence needed to prove his theory. By the 1970s, continental drift was accepted as science fact.

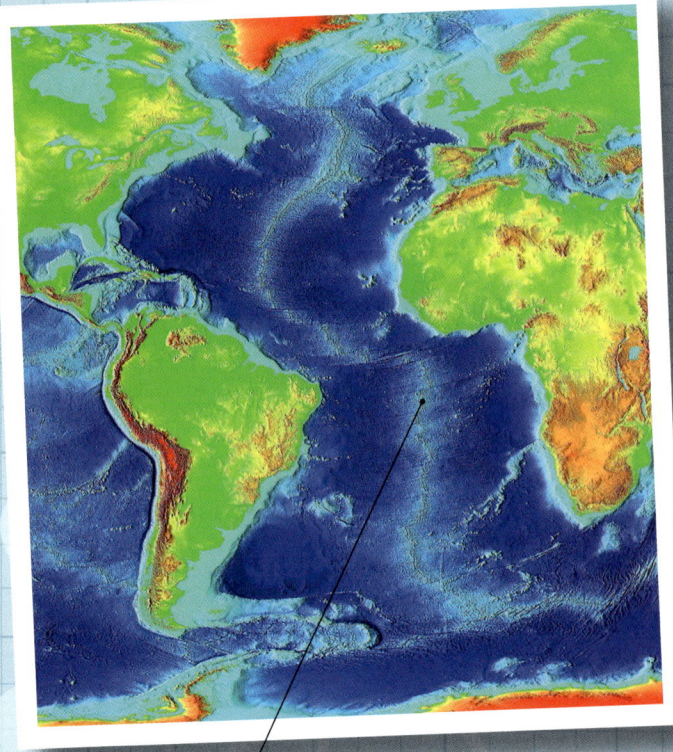

The Mid-Atlantic Ridge runs roughly halfway between the Americas and Europe and Africa, suggesting these continents were once connected.

Mid-Atlantic Ridge

Challenging Assumptions

Peer review is an important step in the scientific process to ensure that new discoveries are supported by testable evidence. Though some theories can take time before they are accepted, peer review ensures that results aren't biased by outside interests. In theory, once enough evidence is gathered and tested, scientists agree that a theory is, in fact, fact.

From the Field: Dallas Abbott

In 2003, Columbia University geologist Dallas Abbot and her team argued that they had discovered the site of a meteor strike that the world had missed. The strike, they stated, took place around the 15th century, 74.5 miles (120 kilometers) south of New Zealand. Their evidence included the oral history of Indigenous peoples, who describe leaving the south coast of New Zealand due to a tsunami, and the extinction of local bird and animal species. A sonar map of the ocean floor in the area also showed what looked like a large crater. Abbot's discovery is still being debated and peer reviewed by scientists, some of whom offer other evidence to explain the tsunami.

Left: Scientific reports are kept in libraries around the world.

Right: Geological features like this giant crater called the "Eye of the Sahara" create much debate. Some believe it was formed by an ancient volcano. Others think it is the result of an asteroid strike.

25

INVESTIGATING LANDSLIDES

Geology is the study of the world around us, and we can study geology at home, using the techniques scientists use. Ask a question, make a hypothesis, and plan an investigation. Test your hypothesis by observing, making models, and analyzing data. Based on the data, you can then reach a conclusion. Try it yourself.

The Angle of Repose

Another natural disaster geologists study is the landslide. Why do slopes of rock give way and slide down, crushing everything in their way? Geologists have calculated something called the **angle of repose**. Slopes have a natural angle, depending on what they are made of, and slopes that have a steeper angle will likely slide. So, what difference do different materials make to the angle of repose? That's a question you can investigate.

What would your hypothesis be? Do larger, coarser materials have a steeper angle of repose than smaller, finer materials? How would you test this? Could you make a model using small materials like sugar and sand? How could you show the different angles of repose?

The eroded material that forms angled mounds at the bottom of cliffs is known as talus.

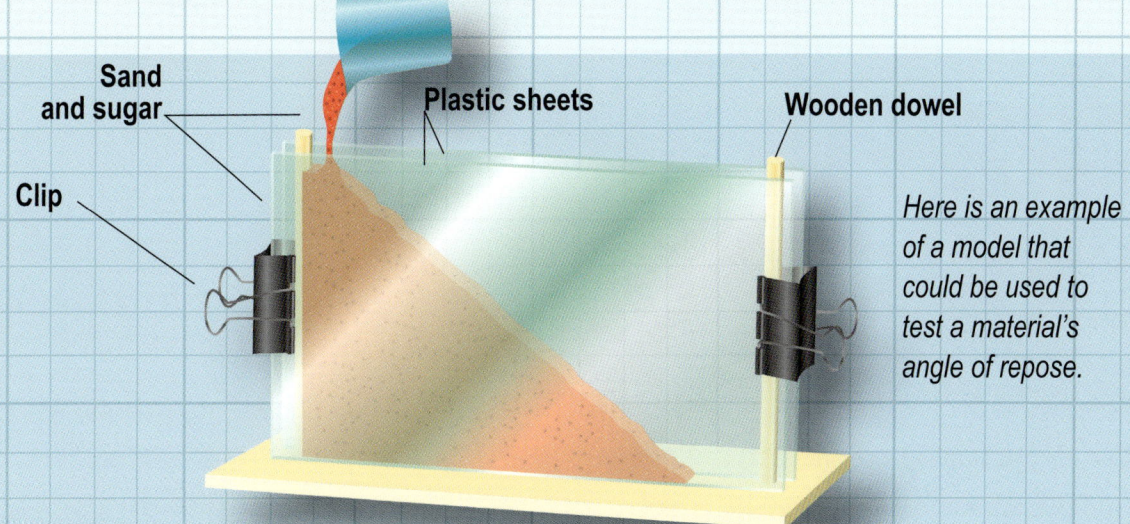

Here is an example of a model that could be used to test a material's angle of repose.

A Possible Model

Your model could use two sheets of clear plastic separated by two wooden dowels at each end. This would create a long thin container that you can pour the sugar and sand into. The sand and sugar will heap up against the plastic. You can then look inside the mound to see how the sand and sugar are sliding and interacting.

Now gather and record your data. You can measure the degree of the landslide's slope using a protractor. Does smaller, finer-grained sand have a different angle of repose than larger, coarser-grained sugar? What happens when you mix the two together and pour it out? Did the data support or contradict your hypothesis?

Don't forget to write a report on your results, noting the conclusions you have reached. Maybe you could present it to your teachers and classmates, and ask them to repeat your experiment. Do their tests back up your results, or do they challenge your findings?

Always Asking, Always Learning

And here's something else. When you pour your sand and sugar mixture, do you notice how the sand and sugar suddenly separate into layers? This is called **spontaneous stratification**. This has only been studied and partly understood in the past 15 years, but it could affect geologists' understanding of how rock layers form.

It's another example of how some answers lead to more questions and more investigations. This is how scientists like geologists learn about the world around them, and they don't stop. Keep looking for answers and finding new questions, and you too can expand your understanding and think like a scientist.

THE FUTURE OF THE FIELD

Geology has changed how we understand the world. We can find natural resources buried deep underground. We are better prepared for the disasters that earthquakes and volcanoes cause. However, there is more to discover, and these discoveries promise big changes.

Saving People and the Planet

When geologists learned that certain seismic waves travel faster than others, this helped engineers set up early warning systems to trip alarms, send text alerts, and open fire station doors ahead of an earthquake. These few seconds of warning have saved lives. However, geologists continue to investigate the forces behind earthquakes in the hope that they can provide even more warning and save more lives.

Geologists are also important in the fight against climate change. Geologists who examine the ice sheets and the ground beneath them are providing vital information about how quickly Earth's climate can change. Other geologists are looking at the layers of rock around oil and gas wells, to see if carbon dioxide can be pumped into these wells, removing the harmful gas from the atmosphere. This knowledge will help us understand more about the dangers posed by climate change, and how we could overcome them.

Geologists monitor seismic activity near Santiago in Chile. They hope to predict earthquakes that could destroy the city.

28

Get Involved

You can expand your knowledge and gain real-world scientific experience by helping out geologists right now. The University of Oklahoma is running a Citizen Science Soil Collection Program, asking people around the world to collect a scoop of soil from their backyards and send it to the university. Geologists will analyze the samples, note where they were taken, and use them to build maps showing what microorganisms living in the ground can be found, all around the world. More information can be found at www.whatisinyourbackyard.org.

Geology students identify minerals in their rock samples.

The U.S. Geological Survey National Earthquake Information Center is asking for anybody who has felt an earthquake to report their findings through a website called *Did You Feel It?* The University of California, Riverside is lending or selling sensors to schools so that students can measure earthquakes. Other citizen-science projects are being set up by libraries, universities, and governments around the world. Ask your teachers or librarians about events near you.

Geology on Other Planets

The future for geology could even be in outer space. Geological patterns on other planets suggest that some processes that have occurred on Earth also took place elsewhere. This could help in our search for life on other planets. Geologists may find water and other natural resources to support the building of space **colonies**. With new technologies and ongoing discoveries, there are no limits to what geologists can do in the future for the planet and its people.

NASA is looking at robotic systems to send rock samples from Mars back to Earth.

LEARNING MORE

BOOKS

Duffield, Wendell A. *What's So Hot about Volcanoes?* Mountain Press Pub., 2011.

Gray, Susan Heinrichs. *Geology, the Study of Rocks.* Children's Press, 2012.

Romaine, Garret. *Geology Lab for Kids: 52 Projects to Explore Rocks, Gems, Geodes, Fossils, and Other Wonders of the Earth's Surface.* Quarto Pub Group USA, 2017.

Saunders, Craig. *What Is the Theory of Plate Tectonics?* Crabtree Pub., 2011.

Tomecek, Steve, and Carsten, Peter. *National Geographic Kids: Rocks and Minerals.* National Geographic, 2010.

ONLINE

Earthquakes for Kids
https://earthquake.usgs.gov/learn/kids
This site helps kids learn about the science of earthquakes, safety, and other cool earthquake facts.

Geology for Kids
www.sciencekids.co.nz/geology.html
This site from New Zealand offers facts about geology and plenty of cool activities. Part of the Science Kids website.

Kids Discover Geology
https://online.kidsdiscover.com/unit/geology
Kids can rock out on geology as part of the Kids Discover website. Video subjects include famous rocks, gemstones, meteors, and the rock cycle.

National Geographic Kids
http://kids.nationalgeographic.com/explore/science/geology-101
This site introduces kids to the subject of geology with videos, games, and quizzes.

GLOSSARY

angle of repose The steepest angle that a sloping surface of loose material can hold without sliding

bias To have preset beliefs and ideas

carbon dioxide A colorless, odorless gas created when burning organic substances like plants, and also breathed out by people and animals

cataclysmic Describes a huge and violent disaster

colony A place that a group of people set up to live in that is far from their original home

core sample A sample of rock shaped like a cylinder, which has been taken out of the ground with a drill

crater A large, bowl-shaped hole in the ground left by an explosion or the impact of a meteorite or an asteroid

current When something flows from one place to another

erode To wear something down through friction

evolution The process by which organisms, through generations, change and develop into different organisms

evidence Proven facts that show that a hypothesis may be true

fault line A break in Earth's crust where tectonic plates move against each other

fossil The remains of a plant or animal that have been turned to stone over a period of millions of years

fossil fuels Sources of energy made from the remains of plants and animals buried under rock millions of years ago, such as oil, coal, and natural gas

fracking A process during which natural gas is extracted by pumping water down an oil well at such high pressure it fractures, or breaks, the surrounding rocks

hypothesis An educated guess at an answer to a question that can then be tested to see whether it is correct or not

ice age A period in Earth's history when the climate was much colder than it is today, and much of the world was covered in ice sheets and glaciers

Indigenous The first inhabitants of a place

interpreting The act of figuring out what something means

iridium A heavy metal that is not usually found in the Earth's crust

magnetic field The area around a magnet that reacts with other magnets, either attracting them or pushing them away

magnetic poles The points where Earth's magnetic field meets the planet's surface. The north and south magnetic poles are relatively close to, but not at the actual North and South Poles of Earth.

mantle The part of Earth, about 1,800 miles (2,900 km) thick, found between the crust and the core

minerals Special types of rocks valued for their usefulness or rarity, like diamonds

model An object or image used to show or explain an idea

organisms Living things like plants and animals

plate tectonics The theory that Earth's crust is broken into plates floating on top of Earth's mantle, carrying the planet's oceans and continents

prehistoric Something that happened before people recorded it in history

satellite An object that orbits a planet, like the moon, or a machine built to look down at the surface of a body in space

sedimentary rock Rock made up of sand and the remains of plants and animals, laid down at the bottom of oceans or lakes over millions of years and changed by heat and pressure into rock

seismic Describes vibrations in Earth's crust caused by earthquakes or explosions

seismographs A device that measures the length and force of earthquakes

sonar A way of measuring how deep something is by sending out sound waves and measuring how long it takes for the echo to return

spectrograph A machine that detects what a substance is made of by measuring the way it reflects and bends light

spontaneous All of a sudden

stratification When something forms into separate layers

theory A hypothesis assumed for the sake of argument or investigation

tree rings Concentric rings found in a cross-section of a tree trunk. Each ring represents a single year's growth for the tree.

tsunami A giant wave of water created by an earthquake or a landslide

INDEX

Abbott, Dallas 25
Agassiz, Louis 9
Alvarez, Walter 21
asteroids 7, 9, 19, 21, 25
Atwater, Brian 15

bias 23, 25
Bretz, J Harlen 19

citizen-science projects 29
climate change 7, 9, 14, 22, 28
continents 8, 24
core samples 16, 18
craters 21, 25
crust 4, 6, 7, 21

dinosaurs 21
drills 14, 16

Earth 4, 5, 6, 7, 8, 9, 12, 14, 16, 18, 19, 20, 21, 22, 28, 29
earthquakes 4, 6, 10, 11, 12, 13, 15, 16, 19, 23, 28, 29
erosion 8, 11, 12, 15, 19, 23, 26

experiments 10, 11, 22, 27

fossil fuels 12
fossils 4, 15, 19
fracking 23

Hirozawa-Reiss, Carol 13
hypotheses 10, 11, 14, 16, 19, 20, 21, 22, 26, 27

ice ages 9

laboratories 10, 21
landslides 4, 7, 26–27
Lyell, Charles 8

minerals 12, 18, 20, 26, 27
models 11, 18, 20, 26, 27
mountains 4, 11, 14, 17, 24

observations 10, 11, 17, 18, 22, 26
oceans 7, 11, 13, 15, 24
oil 12, 16, 19, 20, 28
Oliver, Jack 8
Osterberg, Erich 14

paleontology 7, 21
peer review 24–25
planets 6, 9, 29

Schmitt, Harrison 9
Simpson Stewart, Iain 23
simulations 11
soils 10, 19, 29
Sparks, Stephen 5
spectrographs 17

Tharp, Marie 24
tools 16–17
tsunamis 15, 19, 23, 25

volcanoes 4, 5, 6, 7, 8, 11, 12, 17, 19, 21, 23, 25, 28

water 4, 7, 9, 17, 19, 23, 29
Wegener, Alfred 8, 24

ABOUT THE AUTHOR

James Bow is the author of more than 50 educational books for children and young adults, as well as a novelist and a local columnist. He has a bachelor's degree in environmental sciences.